Matt's

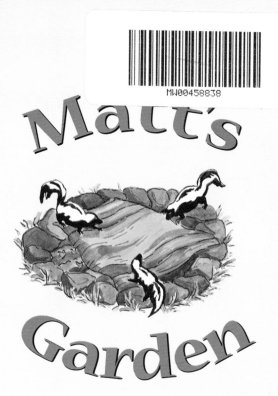

Garden

by Tekla White

illustrated by Marcia Sewall

Scott Foresman

Editorial Offices: Glenview, Illinois • New York, New York
Sales Offices: Reading, Massachusetts • Duluth, Georgia
Glenview, Illinois • Carrollton, Texas • Menlo Park, California

There it was. Right on the front page! Matt picked up the newspaper and raced into the house.

"Aunt Daisy," he shouted. "Look at this! I've got to win this contest. This is the very best bike! I'll never have enough money to buy a bike like this. Could I plant a garden?"

Aunt Daisy read aloud, "The city will award a Lightning Racer bicycle to the student who grows the best garden this summer. On August 15, a photographer will take pictures of the gardens. Judges from the Garden Store will choose the winner."

"My yard won't win any prizes, but it's the
way I like it," said Daisy. "I can sit here and see
rabbits and birds. Listen to those birds sing!"

Aunt Daisy's house was next to a park.
Matt stayed with her while his parents were
at work.

"But if I had that bike, I could go to the store for you. I could run errands!" he said, trying to convince her.

"Growing a garden is so much work," said Daisy. "Have you ever planted one?"

"No," Matt answered. "Have you?"

"Not even a window box," said Daisy. "There's a great deal of work involved. I know the best place to start. Let's go to the library for some books and then we can look in a garden catalog for more ideas."

"A rock garden would be a good idea," said Aunt Daisy. "I've got more rocks in my yard than anything else."

"Look at the tomatoes and carrots in this catalog. How about a garden we can eat?" Matt said.

"A salad is a great idea," said Daisy.

"I'll stack those rocks so they look like a bowl," said Matt. "Then I'll plant vegetable seeds inside. I'll call it 'Matt's Salad Bowl Garden.'"

On Saturday, Matt worked hard. He pulled weeds. He took out rocks. Then he dug holes. Finally, he planted the vegetable seeds. He got blisters on his hands. It felt as if his blisters had blisters. But he was impressed with his work.

When Matt went in for lunch, he looked outside. Birds were flocking around his garden, pecking at the seeds. Matt ran outside waving his hands and yelling.

"You make a great scarecrow," said Aunt Daisy. "To keep all those birds away, you'd have to wave your arms and yell all day."

"We could put a padlock on the garden," Matt said. "But I've got another idea! Instead of becoming a scarecrow, I'll put up a bird feeder. And I'll keep it filled with birdseed. Then maybe the birds will leave the garden seeds alone."

"Yes," said Aunt Daisy. "Let's not get a padlock. Let's get a bird feeder. And we'll put it near the window so I can hear the birds sing. We'll cover the garden with old blankets to protect it while we shop. That way birds can't eat your seeds."

Later, Matt went out to hang the bird feeder. He looked at his garden with amazement and went running back into the house. "Look who is playing with the blankets! I'll take care of the bird feeder later."

Daisy and Matt looked outside. Matt counted six skunk tails.

"I never saw a skunk that close before,"
said Aunt Daisy.

"Close is not my favorite distance from a
skunk," said Matt. "If they decide to move in,
that garden will have to grow without my help."

After the skunks left, Aunt Daisy and Matt
set up the bird feeder.

Then they put a fence around the garden. The rabbits came into the yard. But they couldn't eat the plants. Matt painted a sign and made a big wooden salad fork to hold it up. Then he painted red tulips on the rocks.

"Maybe I have a chance of winning that bicycle," said Matt.

The next day, Matt said, "I have a prize winning zoo, not a prize winning garden!"

Animals had tunneled under the rocks and eaten some carrots.

"Don't give up now," said Aunt Daisy. "We'll put plants that the animals like around the rest of the yard. Maybe that will keep them out of your garden."

On August 15, the photographer and the judges arrived. As they walked out to the garden, they saw two rabbits and a deer.

The photographer took pictures of the animals. The judge inspected the plants.

"A vegetable garden for animals. We're very impressed! Very impressed, indeed!" the judges said as they left.

Then Matt saw the garden photos in the newspaper.

"It looks as if all the gardens are great," said Matt. "I'm impressed. Anyone could win that bicycle."

"I'm the real winner," said Aunt Daisy. "I have so many fresh delicious vegetables. And look outside. They do too!"

Matt looked out the window and laughed. The deer and rabbits were back eating around the edge of the garden. Even if he didn't win the bike, he had a great garden for animals.

All the students were invited to city hall. Matt couldn't wait to find out who had won.

"There are two winners," said the mayor, "Amy's Flag Garden and Matt's Salad Bowl Garden. We only have one bicycle. But we're awarding a new Super Zoom camera to the other winner. One envelope has a picture of the camera. The other has one of the bicycle."

The mayor gave one envelope to Matt and the other to Amy.

Matt cautiously opened his envelope. He wanted the bicycle. But with the camera he could take pictures of the animals that came to visit. He could even take pictures of the skunks—from far away, of course. Matt walked away knowing that either prize would be great. The blisters were well worth it all!